The Seven Sacraments

By REV. L. LOVASIK, S.V.D.

CATHOLIC BOOK PUBLISHING CO.
NEW YORK, N. Y

NIHIL OBSTAT: Daniel V. Flynn, J.C.D., *Censor Librorum*
IMPRIMATUR: ✝ James P. Mahoney, D.D., *Vicar General, Archdiocese of New York*

Jesus Gave His Church Seven Sacraments

THE saving work of Jesus Christ is continued in the Church. Through the gift of the Holy Spirit, the Church enjoys the presence of Jesus and carries on His mission of saving our souls. The Church does this by means of the sacraments which Jesus gave to His Church.

JESUS gave us the Seven Sacraments to make us holy and to give worship to God. The sacraments are:

The Sacraments give us God's grace.

Grace gives us a new life, God's own life. It makes our soul holy and beautiful. It makes us children of God and opens heaven for us. God lives in us through His grace. This new life is called **sanctifying grace.**

God also gives us help — light for our mind and strength for our will, that we may see what is good and do it, and that we may keep away from evil. This grace is called **actual grace.**

Baptism, Confirmation, Penance, Holy Eucharist, Anointing of the Sick, Holy Orders, Matrimony.

Sacraments Are Signs That Give Grace

THE sacraments are like seven rivers of grace flowing from the Savior on the cross, through the Catholic Church. Jesus is our Good Shepherd and we are his sheep. He gives us God's life and help through the grace we receive.

4

JESUS died on the cross to win grace for our souls. The Holy Spirit makes us holy by giving us His grace which we cannot see. The signs of the seven sacraments let us know that God's grace is being given to our soul when we receive the sacrament. We can see the signs with our eyes, but it is only through our faith that we know God's grace is given to us. We believe this on the word of Jesus Himself Who gave us the sacraments so that we might share God's own life through grace.

A SACRAMENT

IS A

CHANNEL

OF GRACE

5

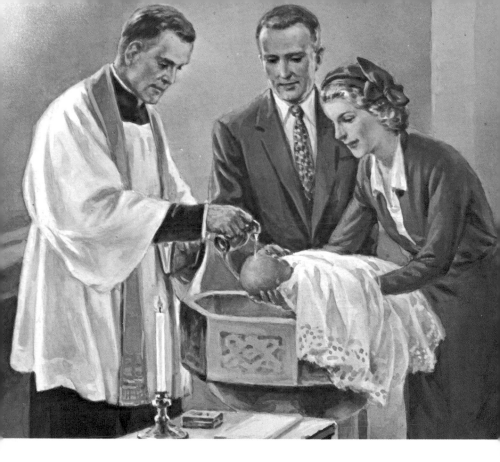

The Sacrament of BAPTISM

BAPTISM is the sacrament of new birth as a child of God. We are made holy by the Holy Spirit because we receive the new life of grace, God's own life.

Baptism takes away original sin, which we got from Adam and Eve. Baptism makes us members of the Church and gives us a right to go to heaven.

BEFORE Jesus went back to heaven, He said to His apostles, "Go and make disciples of all nations. Baptize them in the name of the Father, and of the Son, and of the Holy Spirit."

The priest baptizes by pouring water on the forehead of the person to be baptized and saying the words, "I baptize you in the name of the Father, and of the Son, and of the Holy Spirit."

7

The Sacrament of CONFIRMATION

CONFIRMATION is the sacrament by which we, after being born again in Baptism, now receive the Holy Spirit, the gift of the Father and the Son.

The Holy Spirit comes to our soul in a special way to help us to live a holy life and to be a good example to other people as good Christians.

The bishop is usually the minister of this sacrament as he anoints the forehead and prays for the Seven Gifts of the Holy Spirit.

O N PENTECOST Sunday — ten days after Jesus went up to heaven — He sent the Holy Spirit, the Third Person of the Blessed Trinity.

The Holy Spirit came down on the Apostles and the Blessed Virgin Mary in the form of tongues of fire. A great wind swept through the house where they were praying. The fire means the love of God; the wind means the power of His grace. This was the birthday of the Catholic Church.

The Sacrament of PENANCE

ON THE evening of the day of His Resurrection, Jesus came to the Upper Room where His Apostles were gathered and said to them, "Peace be with you. As the Father has sent Me, so I send you." Then He breathed on them and said, "Receive the Holy Spirit. If you forgive men's sins, they are forgiven them; if you hold them bound, they are held bound." It was then that He gave His Church the sacrament of Penance, and the power to forgive sins.

The Sacrament of Penance brings to us God's merciful forgiveness for sins which we committed after Baptism. Through the priest, who takes His place, Jesus comes to forgive our sins and to give us His peace when we are very sorry for them, sincerely confess them and are willing to make up for them by our prayers and sacrifices.

It is also called the sacrament of Reconciliation, because it helps us to make peace not only with God, but also with people whom we may have hurt. When we go to confession we admit that we are sinners and we ask pardon of God and the Church, because the Church is also wounded by our sins.

The power to forgive sins is a part of the power of the priesthood, to be passed on in the sacrament of Holy Orders till the end of the world. To the sinner who is truly sorry for his sins, the priest says as he raises his hand, "I absolve you from your sins in the name of the Father, and of the Son, and of the Holy Spirit."

WHEN you go to confession, you must:

1. Ask yourself how you have offended God.
2. Be truly sorry for your sins.
3. Make up your mind not to sin again.
4. Tell your sins to the priest.
5. Do the penance the priest gives you.

Sorrow for Sin

THE most important part of confession is sorrow for our sins. We have sorrow or contrition for our sins when we are sorry for them because they have offended the good God, our Father, and when we do not want to commit them again.

You may make an act of contrition in these words:

O my God, I am heartily sorry for having offended You, and I detest all my sins, because of Your punishments, but most of all because they offend You, my God, Who are all-good and deserving of all my love. I firmly resolve, with the help of Your grace, to sin no more and to avoid the near occasions of sin.

13

WE SHOULD have the kind of sorrow which Peter had for his sin. When Jesus was taken prisoner, Peter followed. A slave girl saw Peter sitting among the soldiers, and said, "This man was with Jesus." But he denied it three times.

Peter was so sorry for his sin that he went into the dark and cried with sorrow. Like Saint Peter, we must be sorry, because when we sin we hurt Jesus, our best Friend and our God.

The Sacrament of the HOLY EUCHARIST

JESUS gave us the Holy Eucharist at the Last Supper, the night before He died. When He said, "This is My Body," the bread was changed into His holy Body. When He said, "This is My Blood," the wine was changed into His holy Blood. Then He gave a command: "Do this as a remembrance of Me."

AT THAT moment the Apostles became priests and were given the power to do what Jesus did, to change bread and wine into the Body and Blood of Jesus. They gave this power to other men when they made them priests.

Through the bishop all priests in the Church today receive the power to consecrate, so that people of all times may be present at the Sacrifice of Jesus. The action by which the bread and wine is changed into our Lord's Body and Blood, is called the Mass.

The priest breaks the bread showing that we must all share of the one Body Who is Christ.

The Mass is the Sacrifice of the Cross

THE Eucharistic celebration is carried out in obedience to the words of Jesus at the Last Supper, "Do this in remembrance of Me."

Holy Mass makes present for us the
Passion, Death and Resurrection of Jesus.

THE Holy Mass reminds us of Jesus offering His life for us on the Cross. It is the same Body and Blood which was offered, but now He is in glory and cannot suffer. He continues through all time that offering of Himself on Calvary, and now gives to our souls the graces and merits which He gained for us by His death.

We also remember His Resurrection, by which He conquered death, and His Ascension into heaven to the glory which He wishes to share with us.

The Mass is a sacrifice where the Church not only remembers Jesus, but really brings Him and His death and Resurrection to us so that we may become part of it. Through the hands of priests and in the name of the whole Church the sacrifice of Jesus is offered in the Eucharist in an unbloody — or sacramental — way.

The priest, by the power he received in the sacrament of Holy Orders, acting in the person of Jesus, brings about the Eucharistic Sacrifice, and offers it to God in the name of all the people.

Jesus – Our Gift to God

IN HOLY Mass, through Jesus Christ and the priest at the altar, we **adore** God because He made us; we **thank** Him because He is good to us; we beg Him to **pardon** us because we offended Him; we **ask** Him to help us because we need His grace to save our souls.

In the Mass we offer Jesus to the heavenly Father as the greatest Gift we have, and we ask Him, for the sake of Jesus Who died for us and now offers Himself for us, to forgive our sins and to give us all the graces we need to reach heaven. This Gift is worthy of God, because it is His own Son, offered on the Cross, Who offers Himself now. This is the highest worship we can give God. We must offer Him this perfect Gift especially on Sunday, the Lord's day, the day of the Resurrection of Jesus.

BEFORE going back to heaven Jesus told His Apostles, "Know that I am with you always, until the end of the world!" Jesus is with us always through the Sacrifice of the Mass. Through His priests, He offers Himself again to His heavenly Father in every Holy Mass, and He wants us to offer ourselves with Him — all our work, joy and suffering.

Jesus – God's Gift to Us

HOLY Communion is the action by which we receive the Holy Eucharist — the Body and Blood of Jesus Christ — as spiritual food for our soul. The bread and the wine on the altar remind us of food and drink at a meal. The Eucharist is a meal which reminds us of the Last Supper. In this meal we are united with Jesus and with each other in Jesus, and we prepare ourselves for the everlasting banquet in the heavenly kingdom.

Jesus promised us this heavenly food when He said, "I Myself am the living Bread come down from heaven. If anyone eats this Bread he shall live forever; the Bread I will give is My Flesh, for the life of the world. He who feeds on My Flesh and drinks My Blood has life eternal, and I will raise Him up on the last day. For My Flesh is real food and My Blood real drink. The man who feeds on My Flesh and drinks My Blood remains in Me, and I in him."

In Holy Communion Jesus comes to us as our Friend to visit our soul. He gives us His grace to make our soul pleasing to God and to help us to be good.

IN THE holy Sacrifice of the Mass we give Jesus to the heavenly Father as the best Gift we have. In Holy Communion the heavenly Father gives the best Gift He has — His own loving Son, our God and Savior.

If we really love Jesus we shall receive Him in Holy Communion every time we are at Mass, not only on Sunday, but also during the week if we can.

God With Us

A S THE Ark of the Covenant and the Pillar of Fire were a sign of God's special presence with His people during their long journey through the desert, so Jesus is present with us in the tabernacle to be our help and comfort in our journey through life. God is really with us!

Once people were bringing their little children to Jesus to have Him touch them, but the disciples were scolding them for this. Jesus noticed it and said to them: "Let the children come to Me and do not hinder them. It is to just such as these that the kingdom of God belongs." Then he embraced them and blessed them, placing His hands on them.

JESUS still invites children to come to Him in Holy Communion so that He may bless them and keep them close to His heart. He also invites them to come to pray to Him in the tabernacle, where He is present day and night, praying to His heavenly Father for all of us. Jesus is the best Friend of children.

The Sacrament of ANOINTING OF THE SICK

THE Anointing of the Sick is the sacrament for the seriously ill, infirm and aged. By this anointing with blessed oil and prayers for health, the Church asks God to help the sick in their sufferings, forgive their sins, and bring them to salvation.

The Apostles placed their hands upon certain men whom they picked to be priests, and gave them the powers of the priesthood.

The Sacrament of HOLY ORDERS

AT THE Last Supper Jesus gave to His Church the Holy Sacrifice of the Mass and the sacrament of Holy Orders. He made His Apostles priests when He gave them the command and power to do what He had just done, "Do this in remembrance of Me." This power to offer sacrifice in the name of Jesus and of His Church made the Apostles priests.

On Easter Sunday night, Jesus gave His Apostles the power to forgive sins in His name. "Receive the Holy Spirit. If you forgive men's sins, they are forgiven them; if you hold them bound, they are held bound."

THE Apostles passed their priestly power on to other men in the sacrament of Holy Orders; they ordained more bishops to carry on their work. These bishops ordained other bishops and priests. The power of the priesthood today came from Jesus Himself.

The sacrament of Holy Orders makes certain men more like Jesus Christ, gives them a sacred power to serve the People of God by offering the Sacrifice of the Mass, forgiving sins, and anointing the sick.

The Sacrament of MATRIMONY

MARRIAGE was begun by God, our Creator, in the garden of Paradise, and joined Adam and Eve in a union that could never be broken so that they might love each other and bring children into the world. Their first children were Cain and Abel.

Jesus made marriage a sacrament. He did this to help two people to live together till death in joy or suffering in faithful love, and to take care of the souls of the children God may give them.

Matrimony is the sacrament by which a baptized man and a baptized woman bind themselves for life in marriage and receive the grace to carry out their duties to each other and to their children.

Children must obey their mother and father because they take God's place on earth, and God wants them to love their parents. They owe their life to their parents because their father and mother worked together to bring them into the world. Children should pray for their parents every day.

THERE was a real marriage between the Blessed Virgin Mary and Saint Joseph. Mary was the true mother of Jesus, and Saint Joseph was not His real father, but His foster father. Mary is an example for every wife and mother. Joseph is an example for a Christian husband. Jesus was the joy of the Holy Family. Jesus teaches children how they must honor, obey and love their parents.

Husband and wife administer the Sacrament to each other by giving their consent. This must ordinarily take place before a priest and two witnesses.

29

Jesus, Joy of Families

THE life of the holy Family at Nazareth was a hidden life of prayer and work. They loved God and each other. They were happy together because God was with them.

The life of the Holy Family is an example for all Christian families. Love between the mother and the father of the family for the love of God is the source of the family's love and happiness. Parents and children should give each other a good example and pray each day that God may bless their family as He blessed the Holy Family, Jesus, Mary and Joseph.

A Family Prayer

JESUS, bless our family with the graces of Your sacraments. Help us all to love and obey Your holy laws. Help us to love one another because this is what You want.

Take us all to heaven some day, where we shall be together — as a happy family — forever with God.

Through the grace of the sacraments God lives in our family. The Heavenly Father is our Father. Jesus is our Brother. The Holy Spirit is our Life. Mary is our Mother.

The seven sacraments give us:

1. God's LIFE in Baptism,

2. FORGIVENESS of sins in Penance,

3. FOOD for our soul in the Holy Eucharist,

4. God's STRENGTH in Confirmation,

5. HEALTH AND COMFORT in Anointing of the Sick.

6. PRIESTS in Holy Orders,

7. OUR FAMILY in Matrimony.